T0115363

BOOK ENDORSEMENTS

[✳] *Dr. Willie Eugene Marshall has taken on, tackled, and treated a topic that touches, troubles, and threatens us in total. Difficulties cause us to drop. Problems cause us to pause. Struggles cause us to stop.*

This book, "I Almost Gave Up," educates us, equips us, and enables us with personal experiences, professional evaluations, and passage excerpts to confront the struggle, combat the struggle, and conquer the struggle.

Dr. Jeffrey T. Rainey, Servant
Christian Union Primitive Baptist Church
Mobile, Alabama

[✳] *I endorse this wonderful work by my friend and colleague. May it educate and enhance your ministry.*

Dr. Herman O. Kelly, Jr.
Bethel AME Church and Adjunct Instructor
Pastor and University Instructor
African and African American Studies
Louisiana State University
Baton Rouge, Louisiana

[✳] *To God be all the glory! His word goes out and does not return void. This book is a special 'recipe' to encourage and guide you throughout your life's journey. The joy of the Lord is your strength. This prolific author is blessing you with words to live.*

Reverend Venessa Williams
Associate Pastor
St. Stephens AME Church
Essex, Maryland

✳ *I found the content very relevant to our day to day challenges and interactions. Our constant fight against evil that prevail and the breaking of people's spiritual moral. The Book in itself will certainly help us to understand how we can deal with the issues and challenges but it will ultimately enrich us. The Book does not only focus on the challenges or issues but it guides the reader to understand his or her own struggles and to find a way to deal with it in a spiritual way.*

I thank you,

Johan Claasen
The 15th Episcopal District AME Church
Cape Town, South Africa

✳ *With true passion and real experience, Dr. Marshall gives us hope through one of this year's must-read books "I Almost Gave: Up The struggle is Real." Prepare to be blessed.*

Dr. Rodney D. Smith, Senior Pastor
First African Methodist Church
Oakland, California

✳ *This book is a very timely writing. This country is in the clutches of a deadly pandemic that's festering within a climate of social and political upheaval. This condition is further complicated by the loss of careers, income, homes, health, and life. The government has failed us, church doors are literally closed and hope is fading. The struggle is real and many are on the verge of giving up. This timely writing by Dr. Marshall reminds Christians that with God there is always hope. God will always make a way. God will always make resources like this book available to help humanity. We must listen to God's voice above the clamor of the world and allow Him to guide us safely through the storms of life that will surely come.*

Reverend John P. Gant, M.Div.
Presiding Elder Jackson District
African Methodist Episcopal Zion Church

✳ *Dr. Marshall has a unique way of reaching God's people. God has blessed him to be a prolific encourager and motivator in times like these.*

Charles A. Lewis
Atlanta, Georgia
Presiding Elder Camden District
AME Church | Alabama

✳ *What an interesting, informative, and inspiring literary work. This Book encourages every Christian believer on enhancing their personal walk with the Savior. This is truly a great work on Christian liberation over our trials and our troubles. This Book is practical and profound. You cannot help but to be Blessed by reading it and following its directives. Thank you, Dr. Marshall for allowing God to inspire you and guide you with such a great work.*

May God forever Bless,

Dr. Ywell K. Cunningham, Pastor
Bethel Baptist Church
Monroeville, Alabama

✳ *An inspiring read with practical principles empowering us to know how to live strategically in crisis, through crisis, and beyond crisis. Anne Henning Byfield, Author, "Produced by Strength, Living by Power," Bishop, AME Church.*

Bishop E. Anne Henning Byfield,
Presiding Bishop,
16th Episcopal District
African Methodist Episcopal Church
Post Office Box 55106
Indianapolis, IN 46205-0106
ame16th.org

✳ *Dr. Willie Eugene Marshall has written a dynamic guide leading to understanding the purpose of life's struggles while using God-given tools to overcome them."*

Dr. David W. Green, Sr.
Pastor of St. Stephen A.M.E. Church
Jacksonville, Florida

✳ *Dr. Marshall has provided an insightful, probing and illuminating exposé. This book is raw and real and reveals profound discernment of a believer's struggle to live the tempestuous life as a disciple of Jesus Christ. Thanks be to God, the indwelling of Holy Spirit gives us the tenacity, strength and endurance to defeat the overwhelming urge to simply give up or give out when confronted with life's inevitable challenges.*

The Reverend Dr. Caesar R. Richburg
Pastor, Bethel African Methodist Episcopal Church
Columbia, South Carolina

✳ *Thank you Presiding Elder Willie Eugene Marshall for reminding those of us in ministry of the importance of applying in our own lives what we preach to others: "The struggle is real", but God has provided all we need.*

Bishop Carolyn Tyler Guidry
African Methodist Episcopal Church

⊛ *Obstacles in life only have two purposes: either to break you or make you! Dr. Marshall gives practical biblical insight on how to thrive when the inevitable happens… giving up is not an option!*

Rev. Dr. Agnes M. Lover, Pastor
St. Paul AME Church
Montgomery, Alabama

I ALMOST GAVE UP

THE STRUGGLE IS REAL

WILLIE EUGENE MARSHALL

authorHOUSE®

AuthorHouse™
1663 Liberty Drive
Bloomington, IN 47403
www.authorhouse.com
Phone: 833-262-8899

Published by AuthorHouse 04/12/2021

ISBN: 978-1-6655-2245-8 (sc)
ISBN: 978-1-6655-2244-1 (e)

Print information available on the last page.

Any people depicted in stock imagery provided by Getty Images are models, and such images are being used for illustrative purposes only. Certain stock imagery © Getty Images.

This book is printed on acid-free paper.

All scriptures were taken from the King James Version of the Bible.

CONTENTS

DEDICATION

To everybody in the world who has ever felt like giving up
and maybe have already given up. Remember to stay Safe,
Focused, Positive and Encouraged!

Introduction

"LIFE IS GOING TO MOVE FORWARD WITH US OR WITHOUT US."

I just believe all of us has had at least a split-second experience with the uncomfortable and depressive thought of giving up.

Especially when we encounter one unexpected storm after another unexpected storm.

These destructive vampires of spiritual warfare are real and they still exist as we speak. The careless mistake we make sometimes is when we do not properly suit ourselves with the whole armour of God.

If the enemy can enter the doors of our cognitive flow, our thoughts, then it will give the devil more footage to start operating in our hearts.

This is when the enemy has a better chance to inject a slow killing poison into our hearts that will eventually cause us to feel like giving up.

In this life, I have learned through my personal walk, it is normal to feel like giving up. We might give out but work hard to never ever give up!

I can remember hearing my parents, the late Reverend James Marshall (Presiding Elder) and Mother Lucy Ree Watts Marshall (a licensed Exhorter) in the African

Methodist Episcopal Church, sharing with me proven words of wisdom. They believe with conviction the "School of Hard Knocks," which is our life experiences, is the best lesson designed for any of us to learn how to overcome the devilish tactics by the enemy that can and will, "Make Us Feel Like Giving Up: The Struggle is Real."

According to the Ed Scott article entitled, "The struggle is real, and that's why you need it."[1]

Scott highlights: To struggle is to resist restraint, to push back against limitation. To struggle is to make the difficult and costly decision "to be," rather than copping out and deciding "not to be. The struggle is to show up, to put your best foot forward, to grind and to suffer and to assess, to decide and discern and re-evaluate, to discuss and debate and criticize and be criticized and move forward, constantly, despite or perhaps because of the fact that in the end, you have zero chance of making it out of this alive, and you know it. Because, really, what other option do you have?

The struggle is real, and that's why you need it.

The struggle is a real 24/7, 52 weeks, 365 days a year including a leap year spiritual wrestling match between good and evil. Our spiritual opposition is not a made up, racist, biased being who will only allow a certain people to go through their struggles.

It doesn't matter at all to the enemy about race, gender,

age, color, creed, geographical location, political party, level of prestige, rich or poor. Everybody, as long as we are living, human beings on this planet earth, will come against our struggling giants.

When, not if, we are assaulted by the devil, through trial and error, God has taught me not to allow the enemy to conquer but to be determined, with the help of God, to handle my struggles.

In my opinion, the Apostle Paul gives us one of the best prescriptions in Ephesians 6:11-12:

"Put on all the armor that God gives, so you can defend yourself against the devil's tricks. We are not fighting against humans. We are fighting against forces and authorities and against rulers of darkness and powers in the spiritual world."[2]

This biblical recipe is guaranteed to work for any of us in God's will and His appointed time.

In the prophetic words of Dr. Martin Luther King, Jr., "Change does not roll in on the wheels of inevitability, but comes through continuous struggle. And so, we must straighten our backs and work for our freedom. A man can't ride you unless your back is bent."[3]

This book will cover the following 5 parts:

1. Post-Traumatic Stress Disorder (PSTD) in the Church
2. When the Counselor Needs Counseling

PART 1

FROM THE HEARTS OF KIMBERLY AND JOSHUA

Hello, I am Kimberly Renee Huggins Marshall, and I am sharing my thoughts regarding my life as part of the Clergy Family and Pastoral family growing up in the church all my life. I have been what you called a PK (Preacher's Kid). I have lived in parsonages across the Ninth Episcopal District in the state of Alabama for most of my life. I had a great childhood, my parents were supportive and as far as the church goes, I love the church with all my heart. There is absolutely nothing I would not do to help my church.

Over the years dealing with and being deeply stabbed with church hurt, it has conditioned me not to get too close some church members, but it does not mean that I should not be friendly and to love them.

I have learned the hard way that there are certain things you should not tell church members about your family. Our family, I, dad, and Joshua are our immediate household.

A lot of times, I am not really an argumentative type of person in public. I do not like drama and when I get upset,

I just shut down and I just go into my room, go into that private room and I pray, and I ask God to give me some type of guidance. Church hurt, I have learned to pray about it and to let God handle it. I have learned not to let church consume every fiber in my life.

Even though, I know that church is exceedingly difficult because you have people there in the church, believe it or not, they do not want to see the clergy family as well as other church families succeed as well.

A lot of times I feel like in the church many people come to church out of tradition and good religion but the 'body of believers' church is not in them. I say this all the time and people look at me like I am crazy.

You go to work Monday through Friday; Saturday is the day to do whatever you have to do then you go to church on Sunday. It is like a ritual routine where some people leave the church not really getting anything out of the worship experience. This is because you did not bring anything with you because the church is the body of believers.

The church is not the building and sadly too many church members worship the building. I am the type of person to where I always want others, especially our younger Christians, to do better than what I have done. I always try to encourage this generation as well as people to stay with God, the church and to love one another.

God has blessed to where I have had the same job for the last almost 34 years. I do not know what a resume is because I have not had a job interview since I first finished college. I have never missed a paycheck, I have never gotten in trouble at work, I have always been a team player trying to see the best in everyone.

I always believe in helping everyone and I do not like for people to cater to me even though I am the pastor's wife. However, I see myself as a church member married to the pastor of the church. I am going to respect his title regardless of wherever I am because God has placed him as the head of the church and the head of his household.

As my son Joshua would mention to me privately sometimes how he and I can see the pain and hurt in Dr. Marshall but all we can do is to stay together as one, to trust God and to know that through it all we have been so very blessed.

We have never had to go without, and God has always blessed us when times get hard. We have always been together and I love Reverend Dr. W.E. Marshall and I love my son, my teenager Joshua James Marshall who is a super and great child.

My favorite scripture is Psalm 34:8, "O taste and see that the Lord is good, blessed is the man that trusteth in him." No matter the circumstances, all that we can do is trust God. My motto in life is when someone is blessed is to rejoice with them because I know that my blessing is on the way. I always thank God every day for what he is about to do in everybody's lives.

Hello, my name is Joshua Marshall and this is a song I wrote to my dad and mom because I did not want them to give up. They think because I am 15 that I cannot see and feel the hurt, the pain at home and sometimes at church. So, I wrote my parents this simple song because whatever I say matters as well as anybody else.

Trust Go no matter what!

"Do you need a friend?

Call on the name of Jesus and He will make everything better.

Call on Jesus and He will make everything better.

He does it in the mornings, He does it in the evenings, He does it when we are sleeping.

Because you know how God shows His love to everyone around. So, do not be scared, just stand tall, be brave and follow the right path and you will make it.

Just do what is right, keep your mind on God and He will move mountains. Some of us try to rush things but He will come when He wants to. You know He will make a way so just keep on praying because He is always around."

My Dad and Mom told me not to be mad at anybody and not to hold grudges.

Instead, we have focused more on the good and not the bad. Despite all we as a family have had to deal with, God has still blessed us in so many ways:

1. God has helped me and my family to draw closer together and to God.
2. My Dad became Presiding Elder.
3. I am making good grades while in virtual school.
4. We as a family do a devotional reading every night, closing out with the Lord's Prayer.
5. I have grown a lot in many areas of my life.
6. I asked my parents if I was baptized or not? They told me that I was baptized as a baby, but I could not remember because I was too young. I asked my Dad if I could be baptized now so that I could remember it and guess what happened? He and my Mom filled the bathtub up with water in our apartment, blessed the water and baptized me at age 15 on Saturday, January 16, 2021 at 11:04 PM CST, in our apartment in Dothan, Alabama.

In the words of Grandfather, my Dad's late father, Presiding Elder James Marshall, *'son just do your best to do what is right, the best that you can and always remember sometimes Mess can help you.'* I did not look at it that way but in way it has helped us in so many ways.

PART 2

POST-TRAUMATIC STRESS DISORDER (PTSD) IN THE CHURCH

Often times post-traumatic stress disorder is portrayed as a mental disorder that doesn't occur in the church. As though clergy and laity never experience damaging behavior from church-related activities. God's church is a perfect church but we as human being aren't perfect at all.

Romans 3:23 assures us, "For all have sinned, and come short of the glory of God."[1]

Too many times clergy and lay go through some very cut-to-the-white-meat toxic injuries that has been so deeply traumatic in many ways.

Yes, there are people in our churches of all ages who are dealing with post-traumatic stress disorder that wasn't inflicted by their secular activities but by others in the church.

I read a very interesting article that I would like to share by Ben Reed entitled, "Post-Traumatic Church Disorder: 12 Symptoms and 5 Treatments."[2]

Reed says, PTCD (Post-Traumatic Church Disorder) cuts deeply. If there's a place where your spiritual, emotional and physical life should be safe, it is in a local church. But in a PTCD situation, the safety net you should feel there erodes. Finding abuse and traumatic events where a wall of safety and health should exist carves deep wounds on your soul. You may begin to deal with this issue after having been in a local church that is filled with one or more of the following features characterizing its leadership (whether paid staff, volunteer leadership or elders):

- Unhealthy staff culture
- Abusive (spiritual, emotional, verbal, physical or otherwise) leadership
- Unwise leadership decisions
- Controlling
- Constant complaining
- Fighting (open name-calling, character assassination, slander)
- Gossip (behind-closed-door name calling, character assassination, slander)
- Insulated leadership, refusing to be held accountable
- Self-serving shepherds
- Manipulative leadership
- Bullying

Church staff/leadership teams can have these attitudes and behaviors creep in over time. And you'd be foolish to think that one person that's dominated by one of these traits doesn't seep its way into other staff members and into the church at large. One bad apple spoils the bunch, and one bad staffer can spoil the team. These prideful character traits can destroy staff and church morale quicker than just about anything else.

In my own personal experience, when someone is broken to the level of being diagnosed to have post-traumatic stress disorder, or in the church, post-traumatic church disorder, they need more than just to be fixed, they are really hurt and need a complete healing.

QUESTIONS AND ANSWERS

1. Have you or anybody you know ever had to deal with (PTSD) Post-Traumatic Stress Disorder or (PTCD) Post-Traumatic Church Disorder?

_____

_____

_____

_____

_____

_____

_____

2. If Yes, what impact has it had on you and/or your family?

_____

_____

_____

_____

_____

_____

_____

PART 3

WHEN THE COUNSELOR NEEDS COUNSELING

I can remember many years ago while serving a church. A little girl who was about 8 years of age, asked me these words, "Pastor you help so many people, how many people help you?"

I was speechless for a moment and the best answer I could give was, "God helps me." This really opened my eyes to do some major soul searching.

What other persons than my immediate family can I trust enough to really talk to? Who can I trust enough to actually open up to, sharing my personal stuff without being condemned and judged? Who can I talk to in confidence to where I can be totally transparent?

The Apostle Paul in 2 Corinthians 1:3-4 gives us hope:

3 Praise God, the Father of our Lord Jesus Christ! The Father is a merciful God, who always gives us comfort. 4 He comforts us when we are in trouble, so that we can share that same comfort with others in trouble.[1]

When so many clergy and lay leaders pour out so much

into others, other than God, who can we pour our hearts out to so that somebody listens to our problems or when we just need somebody to talk to?

What does the counselor do when the counselor needs counseling? When clergy and laypersons need somebody they can lean on without letting them fall? Without having their personal business all over the city and the world?

I'm reminded of a quote, "No man is a good doctor who has never been sick himself."[2]

We as leaders, both clergy and lay, can't be much help to others when we are messed up and burned out.

Burnout can affect anybody in many ways such as:

- Loss of interest
- Mental, emotional or physical exhaustion from unresolved stress
- Anxiety
- Forgetfulness
- Clinical Depression
- Feeling Empty inside

I would strongly recommend you to do just like I have done for years. Pray that God will send to you the right, called and assigned professional counselor designed just for you. This journey hasn't been sketched out for any of us to make it by ourselves.

QUESTIONS AND ANSWERS

1. As a leader helping others, who do you depend on for support?

_____

_____

_____

_____

_____

_____

_____

2. When was the last time you took a real outing, vacation or sabbatical for some self-care personal resting time?

_____

_____

_____

_____

_____

_____

_____

PART 4

HOW SPIRITUALITY, MEDICINE AND THERAPY WORK TOGETHER

A joyful heart is good medicine, but a broken spirit dries up the bones." Proverbs 17:22[1]

I can remember after losing my father, I was assigned to a church that had split because of a very toxic experience. After months and a few years of dealing with a variety of unusual and destructive challenges, I eventually was referred by my primary doctor to seek professional help.

My doctor's lifesaving collaboration with me for about 3 hours was, "you aren't crazy, you just need somebody to talk to!"

This short, caring, seasoned and highly concerned about me doctor best illustrated my unknown and in denial condition in this way: "He said to me, just imagine if I'm holding an onion in my hand. This onion is fully rip on the outside but when we did a deep MRI on the inside this onion had started to slowly decay. If you don't start taking care of the inside of the onion, eventually what's decaying on the inside will destroy the whole onion, which is you from the inside out."

In addition, my doctor told me, "you're also like a vacuum cleaner. You have mastered how to suck in things and store them but you have flunked out at learning how to effectively change your vacuum cleaning bags. If you don't figure how to change your mental bags of anxiety, at some point, your bag will explode internally and you bleed to death without even knowing it."

It wasn't until after I received a reality check that it made sense what was really happening to me.

Yes, I seek a professional therapist not even caring about who did know or who didn't know I was seeing a therapist. All I wanted at this phase of my life was relief, peace of mind and to receive the needed treatment to get better with an intentional personal goal to hopefully get well, whatever that looked and felt like.

I was tired of not being able sleep, I was tired of what I was later diagnosed with as being clinical depression. I was fed up with having panic attacks making me feel like I was going to die.

This is when I had to be willing to learn and become educated on how spiritually, medicine and therapy all work together.

Since then, I have lost all 3 of my siblings:

- Marvin Anthony Marshall at age 40 in 2004!
- Bernard Irvin Marshall at age 50 in 2008!
- Frank James Marshall at age 60 in 2016!

I'm persuaded being more consistent in my prayer and fasting life, taking the right medicines, along with my personal therapist has made a miraculous transformation in my life.

I had to learn to stop tripping, thinking that I was Superman and believing prayer alone was the total prescription. Everybody's journey is different, but for me, God has worked through all of these areas: spirituality, medicine and professional therapy in order for me to have a successful hypothesis outcome.

QUESTIONS AND ANSWERS

1. What's your opinion on how spirituality, medicine and therapy can work together?

_____

_____

_____

_____

_____

_____

_____

PART 5

LEARN HOW TO LISTEN ABOVE THE NOISE

From time to time, just like all of us, we will have to be on stage with some church soap opera drama. Throughout my 34 years of pastoral ministry which has been more positive than negative, I have had to learn the hard way, no matter how good you are, somebody isn't going to like you or support you.

For instance, in the midst of all of my successful ministry, not that I haven't done anything wrong by word, thought and deed, because I, too, have made mistakes in my life and while in ministry, I can sadly remember on several occasions when laity have mistreated clergy, clergy have mistreated laity, clergy have mistreated clergy and laity have mistreated laity as though it was just nothing and the conditioned order of the day.

I can remember the words of a wise leader who said, "while people are saying they don't want you, they sometimes forget the feeling can also be mutual. That same pastor may not want them either!"

Unfortunately, people will act more out of emotions with an organized premeditated street gang mentality to come together for an unholy common cause making decisions for others who may not feel the same way they feel about leadership.

These kinds of bullied decision making can bring major harm to a church congregation. It can and will create super division and more lack of trust between others who have been left out of the major decision making on purpose for the church body as a whole.

In other words, y'all just pay us your money, show up and even if you have the right to make decisions in our church, that will only happen when we decide that you can. This is having more of a Trump philosophy of not being convinced that they are rapidly killing and holding the congregation hostage from the inside out.

In addition, I can really say that every mistreatment by others has helped us as a family to grow to be better prepared for the storms yet to come in our ministry.

Remember the Bible applies to all of us, both clergy and laity. "Be not deceived; God is not mocked: for whatsoever a man soweth, that shall he also reap." Galatians 6:71.[1]

Ask God to show you how to Master the art of listening "Above the Noise," and don't say a word because you need to hear and to see the true hearts of the people.

It can be super hard to maintain your cool, especially with people saying the rule is, you do as I say and not as I do.

We still must find a place to forgive even when people don't believe that you have forgiven them all and have moved on.

I can remember on one painful occasion going through a hard, disrespectful and abusive time at a certain church when God was speaking to me in the deepest parts of my soul, "Luke 23:34, But Jesus was saying, "Father, forgive them; for they do not know what they are doing." And they cast lots, dividing up His garments among themselves."[2]

Because of my respect for God, for others and my desire to encourage and not to divide, I dare not list any names and the cruel and damaging incidents and/or words that were expressed to myself and my family while experiencing such inhumane Crucifixion behaviors from and by people who represent the church.

The church is still the best place for all of us despite our sometimes-spiritual wickedness. Often times good people will say and do ungodly things.

This doesn't mean church folks are bad people. I believe there is good in everybody. These unanticipated satanic attacks convincingly showed me how the spirit of the devil can work in and through any of us, if we aren't properly connected to the True vine, Jesus.

It is so amazing how the in-your-face "MANURE" can and has given me and my family so much more eye-opening realities for fruitful growth. When listening above the noise, I had to learn how to be firm while still keeping my cool and being calm so that I could hear from God, and see what God wanted me to hear and to see.

As crazy as it can be, sometimes "CRAP" can help you! One person's trash can be somebody else's treasure.

This process reminds me of the lyrics by country and pop singer Kenny Rogers:

"You've got to know when to hold 'em
Know when to fold 'em
Know when to walk away
And know when to run
You never count your money
When you're sittin' at the table
There'll be time enough for countin'
When the dealin's done."[3]

My Mother would always say to me, Son, sometimes you have condition yourself, "To Listen Above the Noise!"

Romans 8:35-39 had really been helpful to me, no matter the storm, to walk in love, to walk in forgiveness whether unexpected and/or expected in such venomous circumstances:

"Who shall separate us from the love of Christ? shall tribulation, or distress, or persecution, or famine, or nakedness, or peril, or sword?

As it is written, For thy sake we are killed all the day long; we are accounted as sheep for the slaughter.

Nay, in all these things we are more than conquerors through him that loved us.

For I am persuaded, that neither death, nor life, nor angels, nor principalities, nor powers, nor things present, nor things to come, Nor height, nor depth, nor any other creature, shall be able to separate us from the love of God, which is in Christ Jesus our Lord."[4]

My family and I have learned "How to Listen Above the Noise" when people beat us down with their petty but real episode that doesn't feel good at all, especially with things you know you didn't do and/or say.

We can't waste our valuable time chasing behind the paralyzing "BRATTY POO" games of nothingness that lead to more nothingness. We have to protect the dignity and integrity of God's church.

If people don't want you as their leader then there comes a time when God will give you a prophetic commission to walk by faith and not sight; immediate permission to shake the dust off of your shoes and to move on to your next assignment.

Therefore, I have learned through trial and error to always Trust God through the process of trying to be the bigger person.

Because too many times pastors and laity are quietly bleeding and hurting on the inside afraid to share their stories.

Hopefully, the reality of my story will help somebody in a positive way and not discourage! It should always be about clergy and laity working together and not quarreling about stuff that has nothing to do with salvation.

QUESTIONS AND ANSWERS

1. How important do you believe it is for you to listen?

_____

_____

_____

_____

_____

_____

_____

2. What are some of the helpful benefits you can learn from listening?

_____

_____

_____

_____

_____

_____

_____

PART 6

LEARN HOW TO FLY WITH EAGLES AND NOT CHICKENS

Dr. Riggins Earl, Sr., my Ethics and Society Professor at the Interdenominational Theological Center in Atlanta, Georgia, would often remind us in such a prophetic way saying, "if you know anything about feeding chickens in the yard, when you toss the chicken feed on the ground, the chicken feed now becomes mixed up with other junk food on and in the ground that has absolutely no nutritious value for a healthy, productive and successful life.

This doesn't mean to look down on others because everybody is important. But sometimes in order to grow to your God-sent potential, learn how to be secure and flexible enough to fly with eagles. Soar with people who are going somewhere, legally and intentionally pressing their way to a happy and prosperous life."

Sean Smith wrote an article entitled, "Chickens and Eagles,"[1] that best illustrates the difference between the chickens and the eagles.

Smith says, "If you've ever heard me talk before, you may remember me comparing people to a couple of birds – chickens and eagles.

Chickens are flightless birds – they cluck and they hang out in coops. They are useful in that they lay eggs and provide meat (for those who chose to eat it). But most people would not consider chickens elegant, graceful, or inspiring. I refer to average people – those who accept life and have forgotten how to dream and go after what they really want – as chickens.

And then there are eagles – majestic birds, in my opinion, who soar high in the sky with beauty and grace, who see what they want from a great distance and go for it with gusto. I refer to people who are living life according to their terms – people who have dreams and are going after them – people who soar above so many others – as eagles. It's good to be an eagle, and there's nothing wrong with being a chicken – they're different lifestyles and they're for different people.

The funny thing I've noticed though, is that sometimes a person who's a chicken gets tired of being a chicken. Instead of hanging out in the chicken coop, she'd rather be flying high in the sky, like an eagle. So what does she do? Often, she'll ask other chickens how to become an eagle – or maybe just how to fly. They don't know. If they did, they'd be doing it themselves. What she should do is venture out and find an eagle or two – then ask them how to fly.

That's often how people are. We hang out with our friends and family (maybe) and when we realize our life is not as we want it – we complain. Once that gets old, we start to ask questions about how we can change things. Well, the other "chickens" you're hanging around don't know.

They may even feel threatened by your questions as they realize the possibility of you flying the coop, so to speak, if you do get the answers you're looking for. So they may even get in your way as you venture out to try and find the answers. Don't listen to them. Listen to your heart – or your gut – or whatever it is inside of you talking to you – urging you to seek out how you can get more out of life – how you can be more than a chicken."

People will call you all kinds of names but no matter what their investigation results are don't ever allow people to suck the dignity out of the God-calling on your life.

DO NOT LET CHICKENS EAT UP YOUR INTEGRITY!

QUESTIONS AND ANSWERS

1. Do you believe some dreams come true?

_____

_____

_____

_____

_____

_____

_____

2. What are some of your dreams?

_____

_____

_____

_____

_____

_____

_____

3. Do you consider yourself to be a chicken or an eagle?

_____

_____

_____

_____

_____

_____

_____

Conclusion

I fervently pray without ceasing for anybody I'm speaking to in this world. Come what may, I encourage you even though the struggle is real to "NEVER GIVE UP."

"Have faith and trust the process." – Unknown[1]

NOTES

INTRODUCTION

1. https://medium.com/@ejbscott/the-struggle-is-real-and-thats-why-you-need-it-200d80a960ee by Ed Scott: March 15, 2019
2. Ephesians 6:11-12 Contemporary English Version
3. https://www.brainyquote.com/quotes/martin_luther_king_jr_121065

PART #1

1. Romans 3:23 King James Version
2. https://churchleaders.com/smallgroups/small-group-articles/177067-post-traumatic-church-disorder-12-symptoms-and-5-treatments.html by Ben Reed

PART #2

1. 2 Corinthians 1:3-4 Contemporary English Version
2. Quoted at www.picturequotes.com › no-man-i...No man is a good doctor who has never been sick himself | Picture Quotes on 20 August 2020.

PART #3

1. Proverbs 17:22 Christian Standard Version

PART #4

1. Galatians 6:7 King James Version
2. Luke 23:34 New American Standard Bible
3. https://www.songfacts.com/lyrics/kenny-rogers/the-gambler on 20 August 2020.
4. Romans 8:35-39 King James Version

PART #5

1. https://www.coachseansmith.com/chickens-eagles/by by Sean Smith January 27, 2011

CONCLUSION

1. https://www.quotespedia.org/authors/u/unknown/have-faith-and-trust-the-process-unknown/

THE MARSHALL FAMILY

LUCY REE WATTS MARSHALL (My Mother)

About the Authors

Reverend Doctor Willie Eugene Marshall
Presiding Elder, Ozark-Troy District

The Reverend Dr. Willie Eugene Marshall is a native of Peterman, Alabama. He was born in Monroeville, Alabama, the birthplace of the movies "To Kill a Mockingbird" and "Just Mercy."

Dr. Marshall is the son of the late Presiding Elder James Marshall and Mrs. Lucy Ree Watts Marshall. He is a son-in-law of Presiding Elder Willis Huggins, Sr., (Retired, 9th Episcopal District), and the nephew of Presiding Elder Harold Huggins (Retired, 4th Episcopal District).

He is a 1983 graduate of J.F. Shields High School in Beatrice, Alabama, also the alma mater of the former NBA

Superstar, John Drew. Dr. Marshall is a 1988 graduate of Troy University in Troy, Alabama with a Bachelor of Science degree in Criminal Justice, and a minor in General Social Services.

He is a 1993 graduate of the Interdenominational Theological Seminary in Atlanta, Georgia with a Masters of Divinity degree in Christian Education. In 2008 he earned a Doctor of Ministry degree in Leadership Development and Organization Dynamics from United Theological Seminary in Dayton, Ohio.

Dr. Marshall has served as a pastor in the African Methodist Episcopal Church for 34 years, both in the states of Alabama and Missouri. Now he serves as the proud Presiding Elder of the Ozark-Troy District in the Southeast Alabama Annual Conference of the 9th Episcopal District of the AME Church.

He is a published author of two books, *Putting My Stuff in the Past: Healing and Reconciliation*, and *Just Staying Positive: Sermon Outlines.*

Since 2017 Dr. Marshall has served as a Faculty Adjunct Doctoral Co-Mentor at United Theological Seminary in Dayton, Ohio. His co-mentor is Dr. James Elvin Sadler, General Secretary/Auditor of the AME Zion Church in the Doctor of Ministry Focus Group, "Leadership Development and Spiritual Transformation for Healing and Reconciliation."

Dr. Marshall is a member of Kappa Alpha Psi Fraternity,

Inc., a Master Mason, and a member of TA SETI Temple #253, Oasis of Dothan, Desert of Alabama Prince Hall Shrinedom. Dr. Marshall has traveled all over the USA and the world.

For 27 years Dr. Marshall has been happily married to Madam Kimberly Renee Huggins Marshall; together they have one awesome son, Master Joshua James Huggins Marshall.

Dr. Marshall is a candidate for Episcopal Service in the AME Church. The election will take place in 2021 in Orlando, Florida.

Madam Kimberly Renee Huggins Marshall

Madam Kimberly is a native of Birmingham, Alabama. She is the second oldest of 4 siblings to Presiding Elder Willis Huggins, Sr., (Retired) and Lady Hattie Cheatem Huggins, District Consultant (Retired) of the 9th Episcopal District AME Church.

Kimberly is a 1982 graduate of Wenonah High School, Birmingham, Alabama, 1987 graduate of the University of North Alabama in Florence, Alabama with a major in Social Work and a minor in Criminal Justice.

She has been successfully employed with the Social Security Administration Services for the last 34 years.

Madam Kimberly enjoys spending time with family and friends, couponing, movies and traveling.

Master Joshua James Huggins Marshall

Joshua was born in Mobile, Alabama on June 25, 2005. He is a Sophomore at Dothan High School in Dothan, Alabama.

Master Joshua enjoys music, traveling, movies, outside activities, playing his PlayStation and spending time with family and friends.

He is a trained drummer and has been playing since age 5.

Printed in the United States
by Baker & Taylor Publisher Services